Gathered to Serve

Prayers for Parish Leaders

JERRY GALIPEAU

WORLD LIBRARY PUBLICATIONS
The music and liturgy division of J. S. Paluch Company, Inc.
3708 River Road, Suite 400 • Franklin Park, Illinois 60131-2158
800 566-6150 • www.wlpmusic.com

Gathered to Serve

WLP 017350
ISBN 978-1-58459-393-5

Author: Jerry Galipeau
Editor: Michael Novak
Copy Editor: Marcia T. Lucey
Typesetting and Design: Denise C. Durand
Director of Publications: Mary Beth Kunde-Anderson
Production Manager: Deb Johnston

Table of Contents

Prayers for the Liturgical Seasons

Advent

Awaiting the Coming of the Lord 11

The Hour of Joyful Expectation 12

The Promised Reign of Peace....................................13

The Visitation..14

Christmas Season

We Have Seen a Great Light......................................15

You Shall Be Radiant 16

Lent

Forty Days of Repentance 17

Enlighten Our Minds and Hearts 18

Give Us Strength 19

Open Our Hearts..20

Give Us the Spirit of Life 21

Easter Season

He Is Risen 22

The Presence of the Risen Christ 23

The Peace of the Risen Christ....................................24

Mary Magdalene—Disciple to the Disciples 25

The Example of the Apostles 26

The Testimony of Saint Peter.....................................27

Ascension of the Lord

Go and Make Disciples of All Nations 28

Pentecost

Come, Holy Spirit...29

The Most Holy Trinity
In God's Holy Name 30

The Most Holy Body and Blood of Christ
Strengthened by Christ 31

Our Lord Jesus Christ the King
All Peoples Serve Him 32

Prayers for Particular Circumstances

Preparation for a Major Event...................................35
Thanksgiving for a Providential Blessing 36
Prayer in Time of Crisis 37
Parish Leadership Change...38
Discernment of New Leaders 39
Serious Illness of a Parish Leader.............................40
Death of a Parish Leader 41

Prayers Inspired by Scripture Texts

The Spirit Rests on God's Leaders 45
We Find the Lord in Life's Ordinary Moments 46
The Lord Calls Us Today..47
The Beatitudes 48
The House Built on Rock 49
The Call of Matthew 50
The Commissioning of the Twelve 51
Who Do People Say That I Am?...................................52
The Lord's Yoke Is Easy, His Burden Light 53
The Treasure Buried in a Field...................................54
Take Up Your Cross 55
The Greatest Commandment 56

The Parable of the Talents..57

The Separation of the Sheep and the Goats............58

The Call of the Apostles..59

The Healing of Simon's Mother-in-law 60

The Healing of a Paralyzed Man 61

Jesus Calms the Sea 62

The Daughter of Jairus 63

Jesus Sends Out the Twelve, Two by Two...............64

Jesus Feeds the Multitudes 65

The Lord Heals the Deaf Man.....................................66

Who Do You Say That I Am? 67

The Rich Young Man 68

Not to Be Served, But to Serve 69

Bartimaeus, the Blind Man 70

The Greatest Commandment 71

The Widow's Two Small Coins 72

Jesus Unrolls the Scroll in the Synagogue...............73

The Fishermen Leave Their Nets and Follow Jesus 74

Love Your Enemies 75

Jesus Restores the Life
    of the Centurion's Servant 76

The Widow's Dead Son Is Restored to Life..............77

The Lord Appoints the Seventy-two 78

The Good Samaritan..79

Martha and Mary...80

The Giving of the Lord's Prayer 81

Invite All to the Banquet 82

The Prodigal Son...83

The Poor Man Lazarus 84

The Ten Lepers 85

The Wedding at Cana 86

The Woman at the Well 87

"Lord, to Whom Shall We Go?" 88

The Man Born Blind 89

The Raising of Lazarus 90

Let Us Not Be Discouraged 91

Make Us One..92

Faith and Works 93

God Is Love..94

Using the Prayers in this Book

All the prayers in this book are based on one or another passage from scripture. While many of them can stand on their own, you will find that reading the scripture passage enhances the meaning and depth of the prayer.

A good way to use these prayers at a gathering would be:

- Begin with the sign of the cross
- Pray together the brief dialogue
- Have someone proclaim from a Bible the scripture reading that is cited with the prayer
- Pause for silent reflection
- Recite the prayer given (leader or everyone)
- Conclude with the sign of the cross

As you grow in familiarity with this book, you may find additional ways to take advantage of the variety of prayers that are presented here for your use. For example, you may want to add intercessions and the Lord's Prayer, which might be done after the silent reflection. Or you might wish to add a song. And while the prayers are intended for use at the beginning of a meeting or gathering, you might also imagine using one in the middle of a meeting at which perhaps a particular issue has arisen that could be addressed more fruitfully in the context of prayer.

Prayers for the
Liturgical Seasons

Advent

Awaiting the Coming of the Lord

Leader: O come, O come, Emmanuel.
All: **And ransom captive Israel.**

Jeremiah 33:14–16

God of justice,
you who bring order out of chaos,
be with us as we await the coming of your Son.

Inspire us to lead your people with compassion.
Guide our discussions
and keep our love for your people
always before us.
Make us attentive to the wisdom of others
so that we may care for your people
with ever-growing love and devotion.

We ask this in the name of Jesus, your Son,
Emmanuel, who is Lord forever and ever.

Amen.

Advent

The Hour of Joyful Expectation

Leader: O come now, Wisdom from on high,
All: Who orders all things mightily.
Leader: To us the path of knowledge show,
All: And teach us in her ways to go.

Isaiah 11:1–3a, 10

God of wisdom,
you sent your only Son
to be our redeemer and friend.

Be with us in this hour of joyful expectation.
Inspire us to lead those entrusted to our care
   with compassion and kindness.
Open our ears to the wisdom of others
   so that we may serve your holy people
   with a vision that will lead them closer to you.

We ask this in the name of Jesus, your Son,
   Emmanuel, who is Lord forever and ever.

Amen.

Advent

The Promised Reign of Peace

Leader: O come now, Dayspring from on high,
All: **And cheer us by your drawing nigh.**

Micah 5:1, 3–4a

God of day and God of darkness,
   send your Holy Spirit upon us
as we guide and direct the work
      of the holy people
      you have given us to serve.

As we look forward to Christmas,
   make us more aware of your presence
   in those gathered here.
Keep us attentive to the things that really matter.
Help us to lead your people closer
   to your promised reign of peace.

We ask this in the name of Jesus, your Son,
   Emmanuel, who is Lord forever and ever.

Amen.

Advent

The Visitation

Leader: O come, O Rod of Jesse's stem.
All: From every foe deliver them.

Luke 1:39–45

O God of our ancestors,
   our hearts are filled with joy
   in imitation of Elizabeth,
      who greeted Mary with exultation.

As we approach the festival of Christmas,
   guide and direct our actions
   on behalf of the people you entrust to our care.
May our own joy be a sign to them
   of your presence and action among us.

We ask this in the name of Jesus, your Son,
   Emmanuel, who is Lord forever and ever.

Amen.

Christmas Season

We Have Seen a Great Light

Leader: O come, let us adore him.

All: **O come, let us adore him, Christ the Lord.**

Isaiah 9:1, 5–6

God of wonder, God of light,
you sent your Son into the world
to reveal your presence among us.
We rejoice at his coming
and praise and thank you
for the gift of the Incarnation.

Become incarnate once again within each of us
as we strive to lead your people
with wisdom and courage.
In this season of great joy,
inspire us to work tirelessly for justice and peace.

We ask this in the name of your Son, Jesus Christ,
the Prince of Peace, who is Lord forever and ever.

Amen.

Christmas Season

You Shall Be Radiant

Leader: O come, let us adore him.
All: **O come, let us adore him, Christ the Lord.**

Isaiah 60:1–6

O God of wonder and light,
you give us the splendor
of the Christmas season
to show the world the glory of your beloved Son.

Inspire us to share more willingly
the light of his presence
with your beloved sons and daughters
in our parish.
Make us radiate the exuberance of this joyful season.
May our service to your name
truly be an epiphany of hope to your people.

We ask this in the name of your Son,
born of the Virgin Mary.
He is Lord forever and ever.

Amen.

Lent

Forty Days of Repentance

Leader: Draw near, O Lord our God.
All: **Graciously hear us.**

Mark 1:12–15

God of infinite mercy,
be with us as we lead the people
you have entrusted to our care.

During these forty days of repentance,
strengthen your love within our hearts.
As we look forward to the renewal
of our baptismal promises at Easter,
keep our eyes ever fixed on the promise
of the Resurrection.

Give us wisdom during this meeting.
May we discover the presence of Christ your Son
in one another and in the conversations
that unfold among us here.

We ask all of this in the name of the One
whose suffering, death, and resurrection
bring us new life in abundance, Jesus Christ,
who is Lord forever and ever.

Amen.

Lent

Enlighten Our Minds and Hearts

Leader: Draw near, O Lord our God.
All: **Graciously hear us.**

Ephesians 5:8–14

God of love and mercy,
you who dwell in unapproachable light,
be with us in this hour of need.

Enlighten our minds and hearts
so that we may shepherd and guide your people
in ways that bring them closer to you.
In this time of repentance,
fashion our hearts anew.
Inspire us to lead with conviction,
assured of your great love for us.

We ask this in the name of your Son,
Jesus Christ the Redeemer,
who is Lord forever and ever.

Amen.

Lent

Give Us Strength

Leader: Draw near, O Lord our God.
All: Graciously hear us.

Ephesians 2:8–10

Be with us this day,
O God of loving kindness.
You have called each of us
to guide the people
you have given us to serve.

Make us aware of their needs
and give us the strength to respond to them.
In the face of discouragement, lift up our spirits.
In the face of weariness, lift up our hearts.
In the face of great challenges, lift up our strengths.
Give us the wisdom to listen to one another,
that we may lead with hearts attuned
to the needs of all.

We ask this in the name of your Son,
whose passion and death bring salvation
to your people,
Jesus Christ, who is Lord forever and ever.

Amen.

Lent

Open Our Hearts

Leader: Draw near, O Lord our God.
All: Graciously hear us.

2 Corinthians 5:17–21

God of tender mercy,
    guide our deliberations today
    as we continue our Lenten
        journey of repentance.

Help us make decisions
    that will draw those entrusted to our care
    closer to your Son, Jesus Christ.
As we prepare to commemorate
    his passion, death, and resurrection,
    grant us wisdom and understanding.

Open our hearts to his abiding presence,
    for he is Lord, our redeemer,
    forever and ever.

Amen.

Lent

Give Us the Spirit of Life

Leader: Draw near, O Lord our God.
All: Graciously hear us.

Ezekiel 37:12–14

During this season of repentance,
your love reaches into our hearts,
O God of love and mercy.

As we begin this meeting,
help us keep the needs of your people
at the center of our discussions.
When we disagree,
grant us the Spirit's gift of patience.
When we become discouraged,
grant us the Spirit's gift of renewal.
When we become angry or confused,
grant us the Spirit's gift of understanding.
As we near the annual commemoration
of your Son's death and resurrection,
keep our eyes fixed on the One
through whom we have become
your beloved children.

We ask this in his name, Jesus Christ,
who is Lord forever and ever.

Amen.

Easter Season

He Is Risen

Leader: This is the day the Lord has made.
All: Let us be glad and rejoice in it.

John 20:1–9

O God of life and love,
we rejoice in the resurrection
of your Son.

Through the power of his new life,
grant us wisdom during this meeting.
Fill our hearts with Easter hope
as we lead the holy people
you have given us to serve.
Lift us out of graves of division
and make us one in the resurrected Christ,
who is Lord forever and ever.

Amen.

Easter Season

The Presence of the Risen Christ

Leader: This is the day the Lord has made.
All: **Let us be glad and rejoice in it.**

Acts 4:32–35

O God of new life,
    we acknowledge the presence
    of your resurrected Son
    as we gather together in his name.

Grant us the gift of Easter peace
    on this day of gladness.
May our decisions center on what really matters:
    leading those whom you entrust to our care
    into deeper relationship with you.
May your sacred presence fill this room
    with love, respect, and care.

We ask this in his name,
    Jesus Christ the Risen One,
    who is Lord forever and ever.

Amen.

Easter Season

The Peace of the Risen Christ

Leader: This is the day the Lord has made.
All: Let us be glad and rejoice in it.

John 20:19–23

We rejoice with gladness
in this Easter season,
O God of life and love.

May the peaceful presence of your resurrected Son
fill this place as it filled the upper room
where the disciples waited in fear.
Cast out any fear or doubt in our hearts
in this time and in this place.
May our deliberations lead your people closer to you
and to one another.

Acknowledging the presence
of your Holy Spirit in our hearts,
we ask you to listen to our prayer,
voiced in the name of the Risen One,
Christ your Son,
who is Lord forever and ever.

Amen.

Easter Season

Mary Magdalene— Disciple to the Disciples

Leader: This is the day the Lord has made.
All: Let us be glad and rejoice in it.

John 20:11–18

O God of everlasting life,
in this season of joy,
we begin this meeting
to guide and protect the holy people
you entrust to our care.

Like Mary Magdalene,
we come to the empty tomb
and, like her, we discover your presence.
Make us more like this disciple to the disciples
by strengthening us in our resolve
to be strong leaders for your people.
Make us true evangelizers,
willing to share the wonders
of the paschal mystery
with those who seek your presence.

We ask this in the name of the Risen One,
Jesus Christ your Son,
who is Lord forever and ever.

Amen.

Easter Season

The Example of the Apostles

Leader: Give thanks to the Lord who is good.

All: God's love is everlasting.

Acts 5:12–16

O God of life and love,
we have gathered together
in the name of your risen Son, Jesus Christ.
Through the power of the Spirit,
he inspires us in all that we do.

As we look for better ways to serve your holy people,
inspire us by the example
of the apostles of the early church.
By our own actions, draw people more closely to you.
Make us signs of hope for those who despair.
Make us signs of healing
for the sick of mind, body, or spirit.

May our lives radiate the love of the risen Christ,
who is Lord forever and ever.

Amen.

Easter Season

The Testimony of Saint Peter

Leader: Give thanks to the Lord who is good.

All: God's love is everlasting.

Acts 2:14a, 36–41

O God of life,
you have gathered us together
in the name of your Son
to ponder the ways you are calling us
to lead your sons and daughters to new life.

Inspire us by the example
and the preaching of Saint Peter.
Make us unafraid to preach and teach
in ways that are as inspiring as were his ways.
May this holy season of Easter
be a time of renewal for us
as we continue to rejoice
in the resurrection of your Son,
who is the way, the truth, and the life.

He is Lord forever and ever.

Amen.

Ascension of the Lord

Go and Make Disciples of All Nations

Leader: Go and teach all nations, says the Lord.

**All: I am with you always,
                 until the end of the world.**

Matthew 28:16–20

O God of endless ages,
you sent your Son into the world
to bring salvation to your people.
He commissioned his disciples
to go out into the world and preach the Good News.

That commission is extended to us,
baptized in his name.
Inspire us to preach that same Good News
to the people you entrust to our leadership.
Make us aware that the Lord Jesus is with us always.
May we continue to embrace the call
to be true evangelizers in his name.

We ask this through the risen Christ,
who is Lord forever and ever.

Amen.

Pentecost

Come, Holy Spirit

Leader: Come, Holy Spirit, fill the hearts
of your faithful,

All: And kindle in us the fire of your love.

Acts 2:1–4

O God of light and love,
you sent the Holy Spirit upon the disciples,
enabling them to proclaim the mighty deeds
you accomplished through your Son,
Jesus Christ.

Embolden within us the seven-fold gifts
of the Holy Spirit:
wisdom and understanding,
right judgment and courage,
knowledge and reverence,
wonder and awe in your presence.
Help us use these gifts
as this meeting proceeds
so that your people will be led closer to you.

We ask this in the name of your Son,
our Lord Jesus Christ,
who lives and reigns with you and the Holy Spirit,
one God forever and ever.

Amen.

The Most Holy Trinity

In God's Holy Name

Leader: Praise the Holy Trinity, undivided unity.

All: **Holy God, mighty God, God immortal,
be adored.**

Matthew 28:16–20

O God our creator,
we praise and thank you
for your steadfast love.

The communion that exists
among you, your Son, and your Holy Spirit
inspires us to work together in unity.
May our ministry to your holy people
reflect the love shown in the
Holy Trinity of persons,
Father, Son, and Holy Spirit.

You are one God,
forever and ever.

Amen.

The Most Holy Body and Blood of Christ

Strengthened by Christ

Leader: Let us offer praise for the gift of Christ's body and blood.

All: Let us draw strength from the nourishment we receive.

1 Corinthians 11:23–26

O God of life,
you sent your Son,
the Bread of Life,
to be our redeemer and friend.

Strengthen us by his body and blood,
so that we may lead your people with courage
and instill in them a love for the Eucharist.
May our deliberations strengthen us
as the body of Christ.

We ask this in his name,
who is Lord forever and ever.

Amen.

Our Lord Jesus Christ the King

All Peoples Serve Him

Leader: The Lord is king; he is robed in majesty.
All: To him be glory and power for ever.

Daniel 7:13–14

O God of power and might,
you give us the great gift of leadership
of your people here in this parish.

May we look to your Son,
   Jesus Christ the King,
   to be an inspiration for our work and ministry.
When we are tempted to misuse
   the power you entrust to us,
   help us to see in his kingship
   an example of humble service.

Be with us this day,
   as we look for new ways to lead your people
   closer to you through the power
      of your Holy Spirit.

We ask all of this, as we ask all things,
   in the name of your Son,
   who is Lord forever and ever.

Amen.

Prayers for Particular Circumstances

Preparation for a Major Event

Leader: May God, the Lord of mercies, dwell in us.

All: **May the grace of the Holy Spirit
                  cleanse us,
            for we are the temple of God's presence.**

1 Corinthians 3:11, 16–17

O God,
   you are the source of all our strength.
   In your beloved Son, Jesus Christ,
      we have been built into your holy temple.

Send your Holy Spirit upon us,
   to be our helper and guide
   as we prepare for this event in our parish.
May all who participate in it
   grow closer to you.
May they discover your presence
   in the joy they celebrate
   and in the love they share with one another.
May all our preparations bring us
   and all those whom we lead
   into a greater appreciation
   that you are the giver of every good gift.

We ask this through Christ our Lord.

Amen.

Thanksgiving for a Providential Blessing

Leader: Rejoice in the Lord always.
All: **And praise God's holy name.**

Zephaniah 3:14–15

O God of abundant love and mercy,
you have showered us with gifts
beyond measure.

As we gather to ponder the ways
we can lead your people closer to you,
we acknowledge the providential blessing
that you have bestowed on us this day.
We stand in awe before your great love.
We raise our voices in a song of gratitude and praise,
for you have shown once again
that you love us and care for us.

We join our hearts together
in gladness and exultation
as we offer this prayer of great thanksgiving
in the name of your Son Jesus,
your greatest gift to us.
He is Lord forever and ever.

Amen.

Prayer in Time of Crisis

Leader: Be our rock of safety, O God.
All: **Deliver us from every fear.**

2 Samuel 2:1–4

O God of peace,
  we gather here, acknowledging the crisis
  that has arisen in our community.

We feel as if we have nowhere to turn,
  yet we know that at times like this,
  you are our only source of strength and courage.
Help us as we lead your holy people
  through these troubled times.
Make us signs of hope.
Make us signs of your reconciling love.
Make us signs of your concern for your people.

When this crisis subsides,
  as we know it will,
  make us ever stronger
  for having heeded the promptings
  of your Holy Spirit.

We make our prayer in the name of Jesus,
  whose strength we need now more than ever.
He is Lord forever and ever.

Amen.

Parish Leadership Change

Leader: Be our rock of safety, O God.
All: Deliver us from every fear.

2 Samuel 22:2a–4

O God of steadfast love,
sustain us in this time of change.

We acknowledge our fears and hopes
as we face an uncertain future.
Draw us ever closer to you,
our rock of safety,
as we embrace the call
to lead your holy people entrusted to our care.
Strengthen us with your blessed assurance
that we will lead with conviction
and renewed hope.

We ask this in the name of your Son Jesus,
whose abiding presence fills our hearts.
He is Lord forever and ever.

Amen.

Discernment of New Leaders

Leader: Let us live in a manner worthy
of the call we have received.

**All: That we may know the fullness
of Christ's gift in each of us.**

Ephesians 4:1–7, 11–13

We turn to you in our need,
O God of wisdom.

Help us as we search among your holy people
for those who can lead with confidence
and with a spirit of humility.
May the needs of your beloved sons and daughters
be our highest priority
as we discern new leadership.
Give us the insight to discover the different gifts
you have entrusted to the people of our parish.
Through this period of discernment,
may we strive to preserve the unity of the Spirit
and ultimately lead your people closer to you.

We ask all of this in the name of your Son,
who inspires us in all things.
He is Lord forever and ever.

Amen.

Serious Illness of a Parish Leader

Leader: Let our prayer come before you, O God.
All: **Bring healing and comfort to all in need.**

James 5:13–16

O God of healing and great compassion,
    be with us in this time of concern.

Our brother/sister *N.* is seriously ill
    and we join our hearts with his/hers
    in seeking comfort and strength.
As we ask for mercy and healing,
    strengthen us in our resolve
    to lead your people in times of sickness
        and sorrow,
    in times of crisis and despair,
    in times of reconciliation and joy.
Send your Holy Spirit upon us,
    and comfort *N.* with that same Holy Spirit.

We ask this in the name of your Son,
    the healer of every ill,
    Jesus Christ, who is Lord forever and ever.

Amen.

Death of a Parish Leader

Leader: The souls of the just are in the hand of God.
All: **And no torment shall touch them.**

Revelation 14:13

O God of consolation,
our hearts our heavy
and our spirits are weighed down.

We acknowledge our great sense of loss
and we look to you for comfort and solace.
Our friend and colleague *N.* has departed this life.
Welcome him/her into the warmth of your embrace.
Strengthen us to be a sign of consolation and hope
for loved ones left behind.
We know that life is changed, not ended.
Even in times of doubt,
we know that your care reaches
into the depths of our hearts.
May the legacy of *N.* continue to inspire us
to lead your holy people
with love and compassion.

We ask this in the name of the one who came
to destroy sin and death,
your merciful Son, Jesus Christ,
who is Lord forever and ever.

Amen.

Prayers Inspired by Scripture Texts

The Spirit Rests on God's Leaders

Leader: Your name, O Lord, is ever to be praised.

All: **Bestow your Spirit on us all.**

Numbers 11:24–30

O God of faithful love,
    send your Holy Spirit upon us
    as we seek to lead your people closer to you.

Help us to discern your paths
    as you call people to minister in your name.
Keep us humble of heart,
    especially when we cling tightly
      to our own ways,
    ways that sometimes prevent your love
    from being the foundation of our service.
Remove all jealousy from our midst
    and keep our eyes fixed firmly
    on your ever-expanding love.

We ask this in the name of your Son,
    through the power of your Holy Spirit.
You are one God forever and ever.

Amen.

We Find the Lord
in Life's Ordinary Moments

Leader: Open our hearts to listen to your voice,
           O Lord.

All: **That we may know your presence
            in our lives.**

1 Kings 19:9–13a

How wonderful are your ways,
   O God of life and love.
We seek your presence as we come together
   to lead those whom you entrust to our care.

Often we see you in moments of great insight,
   in those times when you show us your Son
   most clearly and most abundantly.
Teach us to seek your presence
   in the moments that seem less important.
Open our eyes to your presence
   in the ordinary times of parish life.
Attune our ears to hear your voice
   in the "tiny whispering sounds"
   that occur each and every day.

We ask this in the name of your Son,
   our Lord Jesus Christ,
   who calls us into communion with you.
You are God forever and ever.

Amen.

The Lord Calls Us Today

Leader: Open our hearts to listen to your voice,
           O Lord.

All: **Strengthen us in our response to your call.**

Isaiah 6:1–8

Holy is your name,
O God, mighty God.
We humbly come before you
    mindful of our own unworthiness,
    mindful of the sin
    that often prevents us
        from serving you faithfully.

Inspire us by the example of the prophets of old,
   who, despite their shortcomings,
   proclaimed the wonders of your love
   to those whom you called them to serve.
Inspire us to echo their response
   as we seek new ways to serve your people.
May the prophet's words be ever
   on our own lips: "Here I am; send me!"

We ask this in the name of your Son,
   who called the disciples
   to lead your holy people.
He is Lord forever and ever.

Amen.

The Beatitudes

Leader: Let us rejoice and be glad.
All: Let God's kingdom come among us.

Matthew 5:1–12a

O God of justice,
   you summon us to care for your people.
   Make the Beatitudes the center of that care.

Make us poor in spirit,
   that others may see your Spirit in us.
Make us hunger and thirst for righteousness,
   that others may see your justice in us.
Make us merciful,
   that others may see the greatness
      of your mercy in us.
Make us clean of heart,
   that others may see more clearly
      your presence in us.
Make us true peacemakers,
   that others will see us as your beloved children.
When we are insulted and persecuted,
   grant us a glimpse of the light
      of your eternal kingdom.

We ask this in the name of Jesus, your beloved Son,
   who is Lord forever and ever.

Amen.

The House Built on Rock

Leader: Let us praise the rock of our salvation.

All: **The Lord, in whom we place all our trust.**

Matthew 7:24–27

God of wisdom and power,
we gather in your name
to lead those whom you entrust to our care.

Strengthen us in our deliberations,
that our decision-making
will be solidly founded on our love for your Son.

Set us on the rock of our salvation,
our Lord Jesus Christ,
who lives and reigns with you and the Holy Spirit,
one God, forever and ever.

Amen.

The Call of Matthew

Leader: Open our hearts to listen to your voice,
           O Lord.

All: **Open our eyes to see your face
in those we meet.**

Matthew 9:9–13

God of mercy and love,
you summoned Matthew, the tax collector,
to be your disciple.

His response to your call
inspires us to listen more attentively to your voice.
You have called us, despite our sinfulness,
to lead your people closer to you.
Continue to call us to deeper union with your Son,
who ate with sinners and tax collectors.
May his actions inspire us to reach out
to all your people.

We ask this in his name,
who is Lord forever and ever.

Amen.

The Commissioning of the Twelve

Leader: Open our hearts to listen to your voice,
   O Lord.

All: Strengthen us in our response to your call.

Matthew 9:37 — 10:1

O God of the harvest,
   you called the twelve apostles
   to share in your mission upon this earth.
We have heard that same call
   and we now rededicate ourselves
   to that same mission.

As we meet this day,
   may your call once again resound in our hearts.
Make us true laborers in your vineyard.
Help us to serve your people with love.
May the harvest we reap
   lead your people one day to eternal life with you.

We ask this in the name of our Lord Jesus Christ,
   your Son, who lives and reigns with you
      and the Holy Spirit,
   one God forever and ever.

Amen.

Who Do People Say That I Am?

Leader: O God, we gather in the name of your Son.
All: **He is the Christ, the Son of the living God.**

Matthew 16:13–19

God of life and love,
your Son called the apostle Peter,
whose confession of faith
    echoes through the ages.

Through the example of Peter,
    the rock upon whom your Church is built,
    inspire us to lead others to deeper faith.
May our work at this gathering
    reflect the love of Christ,
    the Son of the living God.

We make our prayer in his name,
    who is Lord forever and ever.

Amen.

The Lord's Yoke Is Easy, His Burden Light

Leader: We give you praise, Father,
        Lord of heaven and earth.

All: **You have revealed to us
        the mysteries of your kingdom.**

Matthew 11:28–30

O God of love and tender mercy,
    you sent your Son to be
    our redeemer and friend.

Help us to turn to him
    when the demands placed on us by others
    seem too much to bear.
Inspire us to turn to him
    whose yoke is easy,
    whose burden is light.

May our work on behalf of your people
    lead them closer to the One
    who reveals your presence to us each day,
    your Son, who is Lord forever and ever.

Amen.

The Treasure Buried in a Field

Leader:　Open our hearts to the power
　　　　　　of your Holy Spirit.

All:　　**May the Spirit inspire us in thought,
　　　　　word, and deed.**

Matthew 13:44

God without beginning or end,
　we have gathered once again
　to find new ways to lead your people
　　closer to your Son, Jesus Christ.

Open our hearts to discover him in this place.
May we find our lasting treasure in him,
　and be unafraid to share that treasure
　　with those whom you have entrusted to our care.

We ask this in the name of your Son,
　who came to bring us life.
He is Lord forever and ever.

Amen.

Take Up Your Cross

Leader: We adore you, O Christ, and we praise you.

All: **By your holy cross you have
        redeemed the world.**

Matthew 16:24–27

O God of infinite love,
you have called us together
to lead your people to a greater love for you.

Your Son summons each of us to take up our cross
   and follow him.
This is not easy and we look to you for strength.
Help us to bear the cross
   with confidence in your promise of everlasting life.
Strengthen those whom you have given us to serve
   with the same love you showered on your Son.

We make our prayer in his name,
   who is Lord forever and ever.

Amen.

The Greatest Commandment

Leader: The love of God gathers us together.

**All: The love of God inspires us
              to love one another.**

Matthew 22:35–40

God of life,
you command us to love you
and to love one another.

In a particular way
   you call us to love those
   whom you have entrusted to our care.
Strengthen us when we find it difficult
   to love as you command us.
Fill us with charity today
   as we meet to discover ways
   to lead your people closer to you.

We make our prayer in the name of the Lord of love,
   your Son Jesus Christ,
   who lives and reigns with you and the Holy Spirit,
   one God forever and ever.

Amen.

The Parable of the Talents

Leader: The love of God gathers us together.

All: **The love of God brings unity
even in our diversity.**

Matthew 25:14–15, 19–21

Gracious and loving God,
you are the giver of every good gift.
You have entrusted each one of us
with talents to use to build your kingdom
here on earth.

As we gather to ponder ways
to bring your people closer to you,
help us appreciate the many talents among us.
Weave those talents into a tapestry of care,
that we may show others
the many wonders of your presence.
When we are tempted to hide our talents,
strengthen us to give ourselves completely to you.

We ask this in the name of your Son,
who is your eternal gift to us,
Jesus Christ, who is Lord forever and ever.

Amen.

The Separation of the Sheep and the Goats

Leader: O God, open our hearts to your presence.

All: **Keep us mindful of those who hunger
and thirst for justice.**

Matthew 25:31–41

O God, our just judge,
your word challenges us
to fix our eyes on the poor among us.

As we enter our discussions during this gathering,
keep us mindful of the thirsty, the homeless,
the imprisoned, and the hungry.
May our efforts to lead your people
inspire them to become builders of peace and
justice
in your holy name.

We ask this through Christ our Lord.

Amen.

The Call of the Apostles

Leader: O God, open our hearts.
All: Help us to hear your call.

Mark 1:16–20

O God of the ages,
　　you sent your Son into the world
　　to gather the nations
　　into your everlasting kingdom.

He called out the names of ordinary fishermen
　　to become the cornerstones
　　upon which he would build the Church.
Call out our names once again,
　　so that we, too, may be cornerstones
　　　　of your Church,
　　supporting the people you entrust to our care.
Inspire us by the examples of Simon Peter,
　　Andrew, James, and John.

Through their intercession,
　　may we become more like your Son,
　　who is Lord forever and ever.

Amen.

The Healing of Simon's Mother-in-law

Leader: We have gathered in your name,
O God of life and love.

All: **Inspire us to be a sign of healing
for your people.**

Mark 1:29–31

O God of tender mercy,
your Son, our Lord Jesus Christ,
is the everlasting sign of your love.
He went about doing your work,
healing those who suffered.

Bring us closer to your Son
so that we, too, may lead your people
to experience his healing power.
We pray especially for those in our parish
who suffer physical pain.
Wrap them in your healing embrace
and restore them soon to good health.

We ask this in the name of your Son,
the healer of every ill,
who is Lord forever and ever.

Amen.

The Healing of a Paralyzed Man

Leader: We have gathered in your name,
              O God of life and love.

All: **Inspire us to be a sign of healing
              for your people.**

Mark 2:1–12

God of mercy and forgiveness,
we look to you this day for strength.

Make our commitment to serve your people
    as strong as the commitment of the four men
    who lowered their paralyzed friend
    through the hole in the roof
    in order to see the Lord Jesus.
When we become discouraged,
    inspire us by the example
        of these persistent friends.
Help us to bring your people closer to your Son,
    so that they may know his healing and mercy.

Bring us closer in friendship to the One
    who is the source of healing,
    Jesus Christ, who is Lord forever and ever.

Amen.

Jesus Calms the Sea

Leader: O God, we open our hearts
to your presence among us.

All: **Cast away our fears and doubts.**

Mark 4:35–41

God of power and might,
often we feel like the apostles,
tossed about in a boat on rough seas.

When we are criticized,
we can become obstinate.
When our best-laid plans fail,
we can become despondent.
When our programs fall short of our goals,
we can become disillusioned.
Calm our fears and inspire us to lead with confidence.
In times of trouble,
be for us a source of courage and strength.

We make our prayer
in the name of the One who calmed
the stormy seas,
Jesus Christ your Son,
who is Lord forever and ever.

Amen.

The Daughter of Jairus

Leader: We have gathered in your name,
           O God of life and love.

All: **Inspire us to be a sign of healing**
           for your people.

Mark 5:22–24, 35b–43

Gracious God,
we seek your strength this day
as we look for ways
    to bring your people closer to you.

Inspire us by the power of your Son's miracles.
Help us to see in his healing of the daughter of Jairus
    the inspiration for our own work
    on behalf of the people you entrust to our care.
With the crowds who witnessed this miracle,
    let us stand in awe at the marvels
    that your Son has worked.
Let our own ministry also show the marvels
    of your love.
Bring new life to those who are dead through sin,
    and restore them to your friendship.

We make this prayer in the name of your Son,
    the source of love and life,
    who is Lord forever and ever.

Amen.

Jesus Sends Out the Twelve, Two by Two

Leader: You have called us each by name,
O God our strength.

All: **Inspire us to lead your people
with conviction.**

Mark 6:7–13

O God of life,
you sent your Son Jesus into the world
to bring salvation to your people.
He gathered his disciples together
and trained them to share the Good News.

He has gathered us together to do the same.
Inspire us by the example of the disciples.
May we be unafraid to welcome the stranger
or go to places where we are not welcome
in order to share the news of salvation with all.
Strengthen us in our vocation to serve.

We ask this in the name of your Son,
who calls us to serve your people.
He is Lord forever and ever.

Amen.

Jesus Feeds the Multitudes

Leader: You have gathered us together in your name,
O God our strength.

All: **Feed us with an abundance of your love
and mercy.**

Mark 6:34–44

O God of endless mercy,
you look with love
on your people in their need.
As a sign of your care,
your Son fed the multitudes
with a few loaves of bread
and some fish.

We acknowledge our own limitations
in the face of the great tasks you set before us.
Let us not shrink from our response to your call.
May the talents and gifts you have given us
be multiplied time and time again
so that your people may know your abundant love.
May our own meager "loaves and fishes"
be signs of your generous love and mercy
to a people hungering for your presence.

We ask this in the name of your Son,
the everlasting sign of the abundance of your love.
He is Lord forever and ever.

Amen.

The Lord Heals the Deaf Man

Leader: Open our ears to hear your voice, O Lord.

**All: Open our mouths to speak the truth
of the gospel.**

Mark 7:31–37

God of power,
you sent your Son into the world
to heal those who suffer
in mind, body, and spirit.

Inspire us to be signs of healing and reconciliation
to the people you have entrusted to our care.
Open our ears to hear the words of wisdom
that others share with us.
Open our mouths to speak with patience
and understanding.
Make our hearts receptive to the promptings
of your Holy Spirit among us.

We ask this in the name of the One
who opened the ears of the deaf
and the mouths of the mute,
your Son, who is Lord forever and ever.

Amen.

Who Do You Say That I Am?

Leader: Open our hearts to your call to discipleship, O Lord.

All: **Strengthen us as we embrace your cross.**

Mark 8:27–35

O God of love
you sent your only Son into the world
to save us from our sins
and reconcile the world to you.

The cross is an everlasting sign of that love.
Too often we refuse to embrace the cross.
Too often we turn away from its power.

Inspire us today by the words of Saint Peter,
who confessed that Jesus, your Son,
is the Christ, the Savior of the world.
Strengthen us to confess more boldly
our faith in Christ.
Give us the courage to take up the cross
and follow in his footsteps.

We ask this in his name,
the One who died upon the cross for our sins.
He is Lord forever and ever.

Amen.

The Rich Young Man

Leader: Open our ears to your wisdom.

All: **Let us not turn away from the Lord
in sadness,
but seek the Lord with sincere hearts.**

Mark 10:17–27

O God of wisdom,
you summon us to follow your commandments
and to be signs of faithfulness
to those whom you have given us to serve.
When you sent your Son among us,
he called us to go beyond the observance of the law
so that we would draw closer to you in faithful love.

When he summons us to work even harder
to bring about your reign of peace,
inspire us not to turn away in sadness,
but to embrace this summons with courage and joy.

We ask this in the name of your Son,
our Lord Jesus Christ,
who came to save the lost.
He is Lord forever and ever.

Amen.

Not to Be Served, But to Serve

Leader: In humility we seek your wisdom, O Lord.
All: **Grant us sincerity of heart.**

Mark 10:35–45

O God of mercy,
   you have gathered us in this place
   to serve the holy people
   you entrust to our care.

When we are tempted to use our authority unwisely,
   grant us the courage and humility
   to surrender in authentic service
      to your call to discipleship.
May we learn what it means to be true servants
   whose aim is to help bring about
      your reign of peace.

We ask this in the name of your Son, Jesus,
   who shows us the way to you.
He is Lord forever and ever.

Amen.

Bartimaeus, the Blind Man

Leader: Open our eyes to see your presence
in one another.

All: **Heal us of sin and division and lead us
closer to you and to each other.**

Mark 10:46–52

O God of life,
your sent your Son into the world
to give sight to the blind
and to heal the brokenhearted.

Lift the veil from our own eyes—
the veil that prevents us from seeing
the real needs of the people
you have given us to serve.
Like Bartimaeus, we cry out to your Son:
"Son of David, have pity on me."
Turn to us and show us your mercy and love.
Open our eyes to see the gifts that each person here
brings to the service of your holy people.

We ask this in the name of your Son,
our Lord Jesus Christ,
the healer of every ill.
He is Lord forever and ever.

Amen.

The Greatest Commandment

Leader: Let us love the Lord our God,
All: **With all our soul, all our mind,
             and all our strength.**

Mark 12:28b–34

O God of power and might,
  you command us to love one another.
  In response to that summons,
  we have gathered here
  to love and serve your holy people.

Strengthen us in our love for neighbor
  and for self.
May the people you entrust to our care
  see in us signs of your everlasting love.
Finally, O God,
  may we learn to love you more—
  with all our understanding,
  all our strength,
  and hearts overflowing with joy.

We ask this in the name of your Son,
  the everlasting sign of life and love,
  Jesus Christ, who is Lord forever and ever.

Amen.

The Widow's Two Small Coins

Leader: We come before the Lord our God,

All: **Called to give of our very selves
for God's holy people.**

Mark 12:41–44

Almighty and everlasting God,
today we ask you for the gift of humility
as we lead the people
you entrust to our care.

When we are tempted to self-righteousness,
inspire us to learn by the example of others
who place themselves entirely in your hands.
Often we seem to have so little to give,
yet even our "two small coins"
can make the difference
in the lives of your people.
Strengthen us in our ministry
and make us humble servants before you
and before one another.

We ask this through Christ our Lord.

Amen.

Jesus Unrolls the Scroll in the Synagogue

Leader: The Spirit of the Lord is upon all of us.

All: The Lord has anointed us to bring glad tidings to the poor.

Luke 4:14–21

O God of justice and mercy,
we gather in the name of your Son,
inspired by his words in the synagogue
at Nazareth.

Unroll the scroll of the prophet Isaiah
in our midst this very day.
May we imitate Christ
by bringing glad tidings to the poor,
by proclaiming liberty to captives,
recovery of sight to the blind,
and freedom to the oppressed.
As we lead your holy people,
may this be a year of favor,
acceptable in your eyes.

We ask this in the name of your Son,
the Savior of the world,
Jesus Christ, who is Lord forever and ever.

Amen.

The Fishermen Leave Their Nets and Follow Jesus

Leader: Open our ears to hear the sound of your call.
All: **O God, refresh us in mind and in spirit.**

Luke 5:1–11

O God of our ancestors,
today we gather as your disciples,
mindful of your constant call to faithfulness.

Inspire us by the story of the call of the fishermen,
who left everything to follow your Son Jesus.
When we are tempted to hold on to power and riches,
loosen our grasp on the things of this world,
so that we may taste of the glory of the next.
May your holy people see in our example
the image of your Son,
who came not to be served,
but to serve.
Through the intercession of those first disciples,
strengthen us to embrace the call to discipleship
more and more with the passing of each day.

We ask this in the name of the One
who asks us to cast our nets into deeper water,
your Son Jesus Christ,
who is Lord forever and ever.

Amen.

Love Your Enemies

Leader: We come together
            through the power of God's love.

All: **We open our hearts to the workings
               of God's Holy Spirit among us.**

Luke 6:27–36

God of immeasurable love,
you sent your Son into the world
to teach your people
and lead them closer to you.

In a world that has lost its way,
    may his words continue to inspire us.
When we are tempted to hate those
        who persecute us,
    remind us once again of the truth of Jesus' words.
May we fashion the swords of hatred
    into plowshares of tolerance and acceptance.
Help us to do good to all the people
    you have entrusted to our care.
Strengthen us to embrace the gospel mandate
    to love our enemies.
Inspire us to show by our example
    your way of love and reconciliation.

We ask this in the name of your Son,
    who came to challenge us to faithful service.
He is Lord forever and ever.

Amen.

Jesus Restores the Life of the Centurion's Servant

Leader: O God, come to us in our need.
All: **Give us new life in your name.**

Luke 7:1–10

O God of healing and strength,
we gather in your holy name
to find new ways to lead your people.

Inspire us by the words and deeds of your Son,
who transformed death into new life.
When we are dead tired,
give us strength to care for ourselves
and for one another.
Lift us up out of our apathy
and restore our faith and trust in you.
May the miracle of the restoration of life
to the servant of the centurion
restore to us a renewed sense of purpose
as we lead those whom you entrust to our care.

We ask this in the name of your Son,
the everlasting sign of your healing and strength.
He is Lord forever and ever.

Amen.

The Widow's Dead Son
Is Restored to Life

Leader: Open our hearts to the wonders of your Son,
            O God of life and love.

All: **May his words and deeds strengthen us.**

Luke 7:11–16

All-powerful God and giver of life,
   we come together once again
   to find ways to bring new life
   to the people you have entrusted to our care.
We marvel at the signs and wonders
   your Son worked among your people.

Help us to see in the story
   of the raising of the widow's son
   an example of the kind of discipleship
   you call us to embrace.
When we encounter people
   who have become lifeless because of
     sin and despair,
   strengthen us to lift them up
   through the power of your Holy Spirit.
Make us signs of new life
   to one another and to your holy people.

We ask this in the name of your Son,
   who gave new life to the widow's dead son
   and returned him to his grateful mother,
   Jesus Christ, who is Lord forever and ever.

Amen.

The Lord Appoints the Seventy-two

Leader: O God, you have called us each by name
             to serve you.

All: **Make us true servants in your sight.**

Luke 10:1–12, 17–20

God of generous love,
we gather in the name of your Son
to discover new ways to lead your people
    into a deeper awareness of the call to discipleship.

Inspire us by the sending out of the seventy-two.
May we embrace both the call
    to go out to all the world and spread the Good News,
    and the call to summon your people to do the same.
When we grow tired along our journey of discipleship,
    refresh us with your words of comfort and assurance.
May we know, especially today,
    that your kingdom is at hand for us.
Help us to shake off the dust of complacency
    so that we may lead those
        whom you entrust to our care
    with renewed strength and vigor.

We ask this in the name of your Son,
    who appointed the seventy-two
        to proclaim your kingdom.
Jesus Christ is Lord forever and ever.

Amen.

The Good Samaritan

Leader: The Holy Spirit has gathered us together
All: **To love the Lord our God**
with our heart, our being,
and with all our strength.

Luke 10:25–37

O God of wonder,
you are the source of strength
for all who put their trust in you.
Your Son Jesus spoke in parables
to teach us new ways of being and acting.

Through the parable of the good Samaritan,
we gain inspiration for our own lives of service.
When we feel "half dead,"
like the man who fell victim to the robbers,
help us to accept the loving care of others.
When we discover people in our care
who are "half dead" through despair and sin,
help us to be good Samaritans for them.
Strengthen us to embrace those
whom we find difficult to love.

Faced with these encounters,
help us to see in them the face of your Son,
in whose name we offer this prayer.
He is Lord forever and ever.

Amen.

Martha and Mary

Leader: The Holy Spirit gathers us together
          in service.

**All: May that same Spirit be with us as we lead
          the people entrusted to our care.**

Luke 10:38–42

O God of generous love,
  we come before you today
  mindful of varied gifts and talents in this room.

Some of us are like the apostle Mary—
  we seem to be more contemplative,
  and prefer to seat ourselves at the feet of your Son.
Some of us are like the apostle Martha—
  we seem to be more industrious,
  busy doing things to lead people to your Son.
Help us to learn from one another.
Help us to complement the gifts
  you so generously shower upon us,
  that we may lead your people
  to lives of prayer and service.
Help us keep our eyes focused on your Son,
  our friend and our brother.

We make our prayer in his name,
  who is Lord forever and ever.

Amen.

The Giving of the Lord's Prayer

Leader: Father in heaven, hallowed be your name.

All: **Forgive us our sins and give us
             our daily bread.**

Luke 11:1–13

Father in heaven,
   we gather in service
   to honor your holy name
   and to ask for our daily bread.

May we be unafraid to turn to you in prayer,
   asking for consolation and strength.
When we are hesitant to turn to you,
   inspire us to knock at the door of your kindness.
When we are afraid to seek your help,
   open the door of your divine assistance.
Help us to see in you the source of our strength
   to minister to those you have given us to serve.
Help us to love them with all our hearts,
   and to forgive them when they sin against us.

We make this prayer in the name of your Son,
   who taught us how to pray as we ought.
He is Lord forever and ever.

Amen.

Invite All to the Banquet

Leader: O God, you invite us to share in a banquet
of service to your holy name.

All: **May we celebrate the many gifts
you have given us.**

Luke 14:1, 7–14

O God of life and love,
you have called us to a life of service
to your holy people.

Inspire us by the words of your Son, Jesus,
who calls us to embrace all people,
rich and poor, healthy and sick.

When we are tempted to serve only those
with whom we get along,
help us to reach beyond our comfort zone.
When we rely on the same people day after day
to do the work of ministry,
help us to look for new people to serve you.
Challenge us to foster the gifts of all your people,
so that we may weave an ever-growing
tapestry of service.

We ask this in the name of your Son
who calls us to faithful service,
Jesus Christ, who is Lord forever and ever.

Amen.

The Prodigal Son

Leader: Direct our minds and our hearts, O God.
All: **Inspire us by the words of your Son.**

Luke 15:11–32

O God of boundless mercy
and generous love,
like a shepherd you seek out the lost.

Inspire us today by the story of the prodigal son.
When we stray from your love,
welcome us back into your fold.
When your people turn away from you,
may we be signs of your generous love,
welcoming them back with open arms.
As we lead those whom you have given us to serve,
keep our eyes fixed on you,
our loving Father who joyfully awaits our return.

We ask this in the name of your Son,
who came to seek out the lost.
He is Lord forever and ever.

Amen.

The Poor Man Lazarus

Leader: O God, we have gathered
            to serve your holy people.

All: **In our weakness, we are made strong.**

Luke 16:19–31

God of tender compassion,
you sent your Son, our Lord Jesus Christ,
to call us to preach the Good News to the poor.

Inspire us by the story of the rich man and Lazarus.
Embolden us to serve the poor
     in our parish and beyond.
We recognize the richness of the gifts
     you have given us.
Help us to see that those gifts entrusted to us
     are meant for service
     to the people you entrust to our care.
Keep our eyes fixed firmly on the heavenly kingdom,
     where Lazarus, the poor man,
     rests in the bosom of Abraham.
Bring us one day to the heavenly banquet,
     where we, too, will rest with Lazarus.

We ask this in the name of your Son,
     the One who came to call us to himself.
He is Lord forever and ever.

Amen.

The Ten Lepers

Leader: Open our hearts to your healing power,
O Lord.

All: **Form us into a people
grateful for your presence.**

Luke 17:11–19

O God of healing and reconciliation,
we gather in your name
to discover new ways to serve your people.

Like the ten lepers who cried to you for mercy,
we turn to you seeking healing and wholeness.
Help us to be signs of healing and reconciliation
to the people you entrust to our care.
When we experience your healing presence
in our parish,
form in us hearts grateful for your many gifts.
We acknowledge your healing presence in this place,
and we seek your strength and mercy.

We ask this in the name of your Son,
who came to restore health to the sick.
He is Lord forever and ever.

Amen.

The Wedding at Cana

Leader: We gather in the name of the one
                who changed water into wine.

All: **Change our hearts, Lord,
                that we may become
                more faithful disciples.**

John 2:1–11

O God of abundant mercy and love,
your Son came into the world
to change hearts hardened by complacency.

Just as he turned water into wine
    at the wedding feast at Cana,
    may he turn any hardened hearts in this place
    into hearts that radiate his merciful love.
Make us unafraid to come before your Son
    with our own fears and limitations.
Fill us with confidence and generosity
    as we find new ways to lead the people
    whom you have given us to serve
    closer to the heavenly feast that knows no end.

We ask this in the name of your Son,
    who turned water into wine,
    Jesus Christ, the worker of miracles.
He is Lord forever and ever.

Amen.

The Woman at the Well

Leader: In our thirst we seek the presence
of the Lord.

All: **May we find in him
a wellspring of everlasting life.**

John 4:5–42

O God of our ancestors,
you sent your only Son into the world
to be living water for all parched by sin.

Inspire us by the story of the woman at the well.
Help us to envision ourselves at that same well,
encountering the Lord who calls us to new life.
May we be signs of living water
to those whom you entrust to our care.
Help us to recognize the deep spiritual thirsts
of your people.
Strengthen us to be wellsprings of life
in their time of need.

We ask this in the name of your Son,
the living water,
Jesus Christ, who is Lord forever and ever.

Amen.

"Lord, to Whom Shall We Go?"

Leader: The Lord Jesus has called us together
in his name.

**All: We turn to him and declare with
Saint Peter, "Master, you have
the words of everlasting life."**

John 6:60–69

O God of abundant goodness,
you sent your Son Jesus
as a sign of your love.

When we are tempted to see our ministry
as too challenging
or too difficult to embrace,
renew us in our commitment to serve you
by showing us the way.
Your Son is the way.
Your Son is the path.
In times of discouragement,
keep our eyes fixed firmly on him.
Strengthen our faith
and make us signs of your love and mercy
to those whom you have given us to serve.

We ask this in the name of your Son,
the Bread of Life,
who feeds us with the finest wheat.
He is Lord forever and ever.

Amen.

The Man Born Blind

Leader: Open our eyes to see your sacred presence
in this place.

All: **Heal us and strengthen our faith.**

John 9:1–41

O God of light,
your Son Jesus healed the blind man,
and exposed the spiritual blindness
of the Pharisees.

We look to your Son today
and we recognize our own spiritual blindness.
Heal us and restore our sight.
Strengthen us in our zeal to be your light
for the people we serve in your name.
When the shadow of sin envelops us,
send the radiant light of your Son
to dispel the darkness
and restore us to your holy light.

We make our prayer in his name,
the light of the world,
who is Lord forever and ever.

Amen.

The Raising of Lazarus

Leader:　The Lord Jesus is the resurrection
　　　　　　　and the life.

All:　　In him we place all our trust.

John 11:1–45

O God of life,
we marvel at the deeds your Son accomplished
to reveal your love.

Help us to see in the story of the raising of Lazarus
　the power of that love.
May we be inspired to raise your holy people
　out of despair and into the hope
　that comes only through faith in you.
Strengthen us to summon them out of tombs of sin
　and help us to be signs of your life and love.

We ask this in the name of your Son,
　who raised Lazarus from the dead.
He is the Lord of life forever and ever.

Amen.

Let Us Not Be Discouraged

Leader: Let us thank God for Jesus Christ,
who intercedes for us.

All: **If God is for us, who can be against us?**

Romans 8:31–39

O God of faithful love,
we know in our hearts
that you are the source
of all goodness and truth.

Often we fall into the trap
of allowing the things of this world
to prevent us from discovering your presence.
We can become mired in our doubt.
We can become paralyzed by our complacency.
Strengthen each and every one of us
to see beyond the obstacles in our ministry.
Help us to realize that nothing can separate us
from the love you have shown us
in Christ Jesus, our beloved Lord.

We ask this in his name,
who is our Savior and Redeemer forever and ever.

Amen.

Make Us One

Leader: We come together
through the power of God's love.

All: **May we be united in the same mind
and in the same purpose.**

1 Corinthians 1:10–17

We come before you, O God,
Father, Son, and Holy Spirit.

Help us to see in the mystery of your trinitarian love
a model for our own ministry.
When we are tempted to rivalry,
remind us of the loving communion
among Father, Son, and Holy Spirit.
When we disagree,
grant us a spirit of patience and understanding.
May our lively exchange of ideas
result in decisions that will benefit your people.

Help us to remember that we belong to you,
our one true God,
in the power of the Holy Spirit,
and in the name of Jesus Christ,
who is Lord forever and ever.

Amen.

Faith and Works

Leader: The Spirit of the Lord is upon all of us.

All: **The Lord has anointed us to bring
glad tidings to the poor.**

James 2:14–17

O God of life and love,
we acknowledge your presence among us.

Strengthen our faith
that we may inspire your holy people
in the ways of gospel love.
Instill in us the realization that
even as we serve our parishioners,
we are each called to take care of the needs
of the poorest of the poor.
Draw us out of any complacency
and make us ready to serve the poor in our midst
and beyond the boundaries of our parish.

We ask this in the name of the One
who preached the Good News to the poor,
Jesus Christ, who is Lord forever and ever.

Amen.

God Is Love

Leader: O God, we open our hearts
          to your presence in our midst

All: **As we acknowledge
       your great love for us.**

1 John 3:1–3

O God of everlasting life,
   draw us in the Spirit's tether of love.
   Help us to see the love you bestow on us
   through the day-to-day lives of the holy people
   you entrust to our care.

As your beloved children,
   we acknowledge our dependence
   on you, the source of all love.
Make us people of hope
   who always turn to you,
   even in times of despair.
We are humbled by your immense care for us,
   manifested by the presence of your Son
   here in our midst.

He is Lord forever and ever.

Amen.

Jerry Galipeau

Jerry Galipeau is Associate Publisher of World Library Publications. Before coming to WLP, he served for fifteen years as Director of Liturgy and Music at parishes in Florida and Illinois. Past chair of the Board of Directors of the North American Forum on the Catechumenate, Jerry is a frequent team member for Forum's institutes. He presents workshops nationally and internationally on the Rite of Christian Initiation of Adults, liturgical spirituality, ritual music, and adult spiritual formation. He is a published author, composer, and recording artist who has authored several books, including *Prayer Services for Parish Life*; *Apprenticed to Christ: Activities for Practicing the Catholic Way of Life*; *We Send You Forth: Dismissals for the RCIA*; and *We Pray to the Lord: Prayers of the Faithful, Years A, B, and C*. He has written articles for *Liturgical Singer*, *Pastoral Music*, *Catechumenate*, *Today's Parish*, and *Church* magazines, among others. He earned a Doctor of Ministry degree with a concentration in liturgical studies from Catholic Theological Union at Chicago in 1999.